WǑW

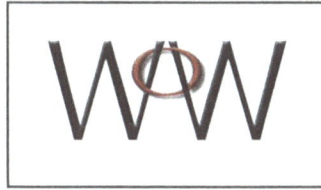

Choosing a
Career as
an Entrepreneur

Working as an entrepreneur can be an exciting and rewarding career path.

WØW

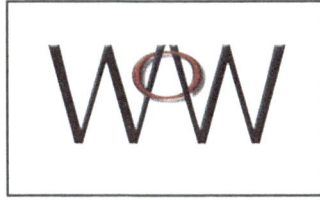

Choosing a Career as an Entrepreneur

Lucy MacGregor

The Rosen Publishing Group, Inc.
New York

Published in 2001 by The Rosen Publishing Group, Inc.
29 East 21st Street, New York, NY 10010

First Edition

Library of Congress Cataloging-in-Publication Data

MacGregor, Lucy.
   Choosing a Career as an Entrepreneur / by Lucy MacGregor.—1st ed.
      p. cm.—(The world of work)
  Includes bibliographical references and index.
  ISBN: 978-1-4358-8688-9
   1. Entrepreneurship. 2. Vocational guidance—United States. I. Title. II. World of work (New York, NY).
  HB615 .M317 2000
  650.14—dc21

                       00-012136

Manufactured in the United States of America

Contents

Introduction

*C*assidy was twenty-one when she began having second thoughts about her career choice. After graduating from college with a degree in communications, she thought that publishing might be the right field for her. She loved books and thought that she had a knack for editing.

After searching for a job for a few months, she finally found a good position with a well-established publishing company. While she enjoyed it at first, eventually Cassidy became less enthusiastic.

"I just couldn't imagine working in publishing my whole life," she says. "I enjoyed editing, and I loved books, but there were certain aspects I didn't like. For one thing, I wasn't sure I liked working for a large corporation. Also, it seemed as though I would have to work there for quite some time before I would get good books to work on. And though these are only little things, I didn't like *the fact that I only had forty-five minutes for lunch, and that I didn't get paid for overtime. After two years I decided that I needed a change."*

While Cassidy was looking for another job, her company announced that it was having financial problems and would have to reduce some staff. Even though Cassidy wasn't one of the people who were laid off, some of her friends lost their jobs.

"That was really hard," Cassidy says now. "Some of my friends—and they were really hard workers too—were laid off from a job they loved. I understood that the company had financial problems, and that it had to reduce staff and make other financial decisions, but this just seemed so unfair to me. I decided then and there that I wanted to work for a smaller publishing house, and one that was doing well financially."

Cassidy went to work for a smaller publishing house—a successful one that was expanding rapidly. There, Cassidy was happy to find that she had more responsibility than she had had at her previous job. Not only did she have more books to edit, she also had the opportunity to manage three people and show them the ropes. Even though she felt like she was closer to what she wanted, Cassidy still didn't think she had hit the nail on the head.

If you think that you want to start your own business, begin by doing plenty of research on your chosen field or skill.

"I still didn't feel as though I was doing what I was meant to do," Cassidy says. "I really liked the people that I worked with, and I loved being their mentor. And while I still liked being an editor, I just didn't feel all that passionate about the work. So I started doing a lot of research and thought a lot about the kind of career I would be best suited for."

After work and on weekends, Cassidy did a lot of research. She took out some career guides from the library and thought a lot about what she wanted from a career, and what kind of position she wanted to have a few years down the road.

"After a lot of thinking I had a clearer idea of what I wanted to do," says Cassidy. "I realized I wanted to start my own consulting business."

Cassidy spent a full summer conferring with her father about what steps to take next.

"My dad started his own business when he was in his mid-twenties," says Cassidy. "So he was able to offer me a lot of help and advice. Together, we discussed the many things I would need to do in order to make my dream a reality.

"Five years later, my consulting business has turned into a profitable venture, and I couldn't be happier."

Perhaps you are like Cassidy—you've spent some time in a job that you thought was a good fit, and now you realize that you have a hidden passion for something else. Or maybe you are still in high school, but dream of ways you can satisfy your entrepreneurial spirit by starting your own business. Whatever the case, you will discover that given the appropriate research, timing, and desire, anyone can be a successful entrepreneur.

Is There a "Right" Time to Become an Entrepreneur?

You can be a successful entrepreneur at any stage in life. Some entrepreneurs are in their thirties, forties, or fifties, and have had years of experience working for a company, but decide to venture out on their own. Others dream of being an entrepreneur at a young age, constantly thinking of new ideas and ways that they can be successful.

It may surprise you to learn that it is possible to be successful at starting your own company or business even if you have little or no experience in the field that you choose to pursue. As an example, many new companies were started by young people in the 1990s during the technology boom.

Zhong Puts His Talents to Use

When he was fifteen, Zhong and his family moved to California from the Guangdong Province in China. Although it took him a while to become fluent in English, he was the best student in his computer class. He

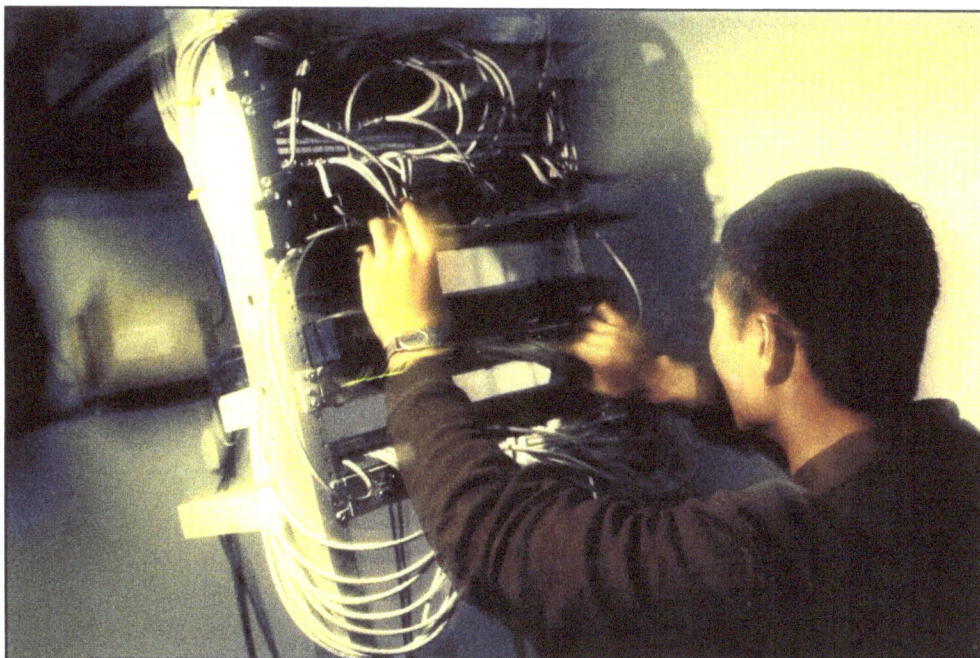

There is always a demand for entrepreneurs in the field of computer programming.

started an after-school computer club with some other students, and he became so involved in writing computer codes that he started to neglect his homework.

In their small town near the beach, Zhong was gaining a reputation for being a real computer whiz. He could crack any code, fix any machine, write any program, and basically do anything computer-related.

One day, the older brother of a friend of Zhong's contacted him and suggested that they meet for lunch on a Saturday. Chaz had a business proposal for Zhong.

"I'll get to the point, Zhong," said Chaz. "I want to start a computer business, but I need a partner. I've got the funds, but not the knowledge. That's where you come in."

"Wow!" exclaimed Zhong. "But I haven't even finished high school yet!"

"I know, but I just wanted to toss out the idea. Why don't you think about it for a week, and get back to me?"

When Zhong went home, he talked to his parents about what Chaz had said. At first his parents said that Zhong had to finish high school, but the more they thought about it, the more they realized this might be the perfect opportunity for their son.

Zhong was cautious at first, but during his week of thinking he realized that high school was getting in the way of what he really wanted to do. And, if this business didn't work, he could always go back to school.

After much consideration, Zhong and his parents decided that this business venture was worth a shot. Zhong and Chaz shook on the deal.

No book can serve as a complete guide to being an entrepreneur—much of what you will need depends on your varied experiences and resources. However, this book will provide you with the foundation to help you uncover your entrepreneurial interests, discover the personal characteristics you need to be successful, and figure out if being an entrepreneur is right for you.

1

What Is an Entrepreneur?

You may be wondering: What exactly is an entrepreneur? An entrepreneur is often defined as one who undertakes an enterprise, like what Cassidy and Zhong did. In other words, an entrepreneur is a person who begins a business or enterprise on his or her own or with a partner.

Who Can Be an Entrepreneur?

Anyone can be an entrepreneur: a construction worker who starts a contracting business; a computer whiz who develops a Web site; a fashion pro who starts a clothing company.

Which type of company you decide to start will largely depend on your interests and skills, and on your available resources. As you can imagine, the decision to start a company should not be taken lightly and is not an easy one to make. To further complicate matters, you must keep in mind that even if you know what kind of company you would like to start, you must also know what type of company has the possibility of becoming successful.

The Options Are Endless

You can also be an entrepreneur without wanting to develop a large company. There are many entrepreneurs who develop businesses just for themselves; they may have plenty of work and accept a lot of new business, but the work is handled on their own. Some people make their business the full focus of their lives; others do it part-time and on the weekends. The options are endless and will vary according to your needs and desires.

Full-Time versus Part-Time Entrepreneurship: Hal's Story

Hal is a twenty-six-year-old from Oakville, Ontario, who wanted to be a full-time entrepreneur.

"I had spent six years working for other people and then I hit a point in my life where I decided that I wanted to work only for myself," Hal says, laughing.

Hal eventually set up an auto repair business working out of his garage. Although it was kind of slow at first, he eventually built up a loyal customer base. Hal had also managed to iron out most of the small things that were keeping the business from running smoothly. Now, two years later, his business is flourishing.

Entrepreneurs can take interests, hobbies, or skills learned elsewhere and apply them to their businesses.

Iris's Story

"When I was thirty, I quit my job so I could stay at home and take care of my two young children," Iris says. *"But I realized that I was missing out on one of my passions: teaching people how to cook. But it was really important to me that my work didn't take over my life."*

Eventually, Iris started a small cooking school, which she ran out of her home. She gave lessons two nights per week and once on the weekends.

"It gave me a nice balance between looking after my kids and doing what I really loved to do," says Iris.

Starting your own business offers a wide variety of choices: whether you want to work part- or full-time, alone or with a partner, at home or in an office.

Whatever the case—whether you want to work part-time or full-time—you can rest assured that you are not the only one who is trying to start your own company. In fact, 11.6 percent of those born in the United States are entrepreneurs. This is terrific news for you up-and-coming entrepreneurs because it means that there are plenty of available resources to help and guide you as you begin your endeavors. From magazine articles to Web sites to support groups and organizations, there is plenty of advice and information available for those interested in starting their own businesses, or those who simply want to learn more about entrepreneurs, who they are, and what they do.

2

Uncovering Your Interests and Choosing the Right Career

Different people have varying reasons for wanting to be entrepreneurs. At a recent gathering of entrepreneurs, people were asked why they wanted to start their own business. The following is a list of the most common answers:

✔ "Because I want to follow in the footsteps of my parents."

✔ "I wanted a change from working for a large corporation."

✔ "I really thought it would be cool to be my own boss, or at least give it a try. That way I could work according to my schedule instead of the old nine-to-five thing."

✔ "Starting my own venture would be a challenge . . . and I was curious to see if I could actually pull it off."

People who are younger and who don't have as much work experience often think that their skills would be useful in a particular market. In other words, they think they have an idea and a way of executing that idea that might be successful and that consumers would be interested in. To use an example, if a person knows how to install storm windows, and a lot of people need to have storm windows installed, it is reasonable to assume that these skills are valuable.

A New Web Site Company

Brad, twenty, recently graduated from college with a graphic design major and a minor in computer science. Brad was especially interested in Web site design.

"I enjoy creating and designing Web sites because that kind of work gives me a chance to use both of my skills—my creativity and my technological savvy," says Brad. *"Because I think that computers are really cool, and because I like graphic design, it's great for me to do this kind of work. I really enjoy it."*

It came as no surprise to Brad's family and friends when he announced, shortly after graduation, that he was planning on beginning his own Web site design company. At first, Brad's parents were a bit skeptical because they felt that he should have more work experience before he ventured out on his own. Besides, he didn't have much money, and they were afraid that he didn't have the skills that starting a business would require. Sure, they knew he had definite talent with Web site design, but they also knew that starting a business required other things: not just money, but strong business skills and contacts.

Brad heeded his parents' advice. He enrolled in an intensive business course that focused on the practical how-to's of starting a business. And while he was taking the course, he decided he would work part-time to earn some extra money. After he completed the course, he felt more ready than ever.

"My parents still weren't convinced," laughed Brad. "But they were willing to stand behind me and support me in any way they could."

Starting a Business—The First Steps

Starting a business requires more than just having an idea. As we saw with Brad, many other elements are involved: money, extensive knowledge of the subject matter, and a business sense, to name just a few. In Brad's case, his interest in Web design had been developing for a few years, so he had a solid idea of what his work would be like, what types of projects he was interested in, and so on.

However, Brad was missing the business knowledge he needed to start his own business plan, and he lacked the appropriate financial backing as

19

Taking courses in other subjects, such as business or accounting, can give an entrepreneur the skills necessary to get his or her idea off the ground.

well. Through the course he took, Brad learned about writing a business plan, setting goals and targets, and creating a business model that would prepare him for the future as his business took shape.

No matter what your strengths and weaknesses are, it is crucial that you have a clear idea of what you are getting into. This includes not only understanding the type of work you will be doing, but also what the day-to-day workload will be like. If Brad had started his company right after he graduated, for example, he would have had a pretty good idea as to the Web site design aspect of his job. But what about the other details? Through his business course, Brad realized he hadn't considered the following:

1. Who would handle the accounting and finances of the business?

Brad was so focused on the Web design aspect of his job—the part that he truly loved—that he neglected to consider who would handle the accounting and finances of his business.

2. How would he attract clients?

Brad realized he hadn't thought about where his clients would come from, or how he would get them.

3. What type of work would he focus on?

Although Brad knew that he wanted to do Web site design, he never stopped to consider the types of projects he would want to work on.

For example, was he interested in designing Web sites for corporate clients? Was there a particular type of business he wanted to do design for, or was he open to anything? Brad's business course forced him to think about some of these things.

4. What type of budget was he working with?

Brad knew he didn't have much money, but he hadn't actually sat down and figured out if he had enough money to make the company work.

5. Was he planning on hiring other people to handle the work? If so, when? How would he be able to pay them? How quickly did he want the business to expand?

Brad realized that he hadn't put much thought into what the business would look like five years down the road.

6. If the business did expand, where was he planning on moving the business to?

Although Brad had envisioned working from his computer at his home, he hadn't thought about how that might change once the company got off the ground.

As you can see, the questions go on and on. While you can never fully prepare for absolutely everything that might crop up, you should try to be as prepared as possible. Remember to try to cover every conceivable aspect of what needs to be done before you begin your venture.

What to Do Next

You may be at the point where you know what kind of business you would like to go into, or you may be at the point where you are just beginning to research a number of careers. If you're not quite sure what type of business you are interested in, there are a number of ways you can find out. Beyond reading about careers, there are many options that can help you get a sense of what you are getting into. Some of these include:

Getting Work Experience

One of the best ways to find out if a particular type of work is suited to you is to actually try it out. There are several ways to do this: part-time or full-time paid work, short-term or long-term volunteer work, or an internship. Work experience is vital for a number of reasons; the most obvious is that the more work experience you have, the easier it will be to start on your entrepreneurial endeavors. Even if you are just volunteering in a particular field a couple of times a week, you will still be able to get a good sense of what the day-to-day work is like.

Networking

Beyond the obvious benefits of getting work experience, you can also gain several key things from your work. Through working, you can develop contacts and referrals to help you create a network of people in that field. This is what is commonly known as networking. Let's look at how Jackie networked to get the job that she wanted.

23

Jackie

Jackie worked in the marketing department of a popular soda company. After Jackie had spent four years in this position, she decided that she needed a change. Jackie began looking for work outside the company, but she didn't find anything that she liked.

"I realized I liked everything about the company that I was working for, but I was bored from working on the same product for four years," she says. "And one day I was telling this to a coworker of mine, and she suggested that I contact James, who worked in marketing for a different division.

"Although I had never worked with James, I had spoken with him a few times at business luncheons. When I went to see him he said that he would let me know when a new position in his group opened up."

Sure enough, James called Jackie a few months later to let her know that there was a marketing position open in the snacks division of the company. To her delight, Jackie got the job.

What Jackie did is called networking—she had never worked with James, but she did know him through social gatherings. In this case, Jackie used her contact—James—to get herself a new job in the division that she wanted to work in.

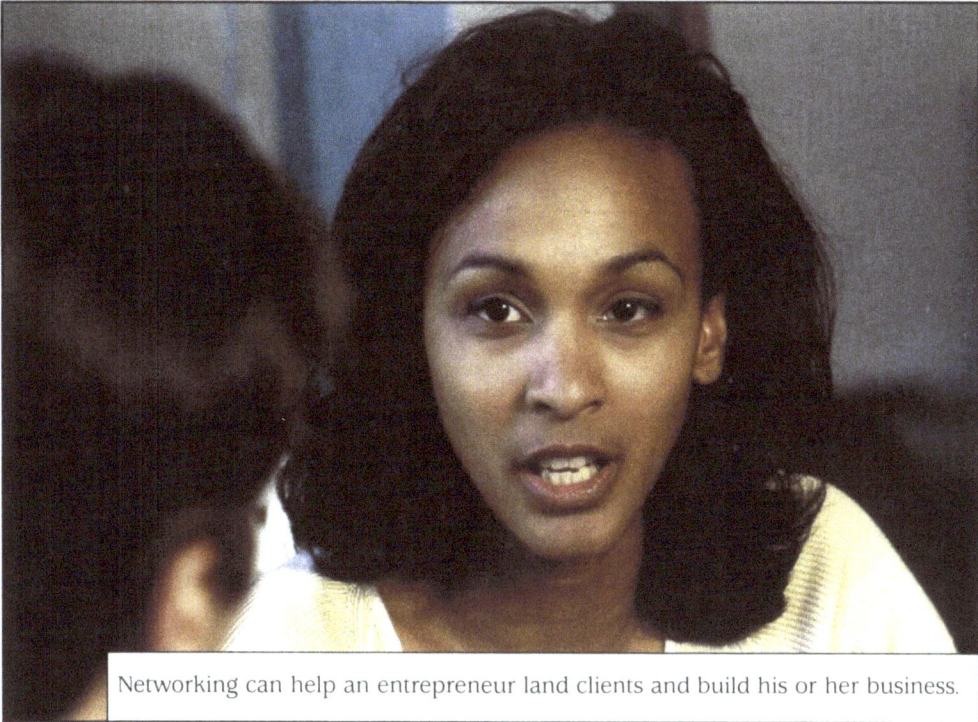
Networking can help an entrepreneur land clients and build his or her business.

In addition to helping you get a new job, networking can also help you in terms of support, since it is always useful to know people who are in the same field as you are. These people can offer advice, share their experiences, and help you out if necessary. Additionally, if you have a strong network of people in your field, you will likely have an easier time getting clients and people interested in hiring you or working with you.

Knowing Your Strengths and Weaknesses

Work experience can also provide you with valuable knowledge about the strengths and weaknesses of your work-related skills. While you may think that you have a good handle on your strengths and weaknesses, putting yourself to the test—that is, working and getting feedback from others—can help you realize what things you are best at and what you need to work on. This is important, because it can give you a chance to play up your strengths and improve your weaknesses. This will, in turn, make your work better.

Developing Lifelong Skills

Working can also help you in other ways. Through interactions with others, you will develop valuable communication skills that will be extremely helpful as you start your new venture. You can also develop leadership skills—if you help hire and mentor other employees, for example—which will help you in many areas. Also, working can provide you with experience in developing analytical, organizational, problem-solving, and creative skills. Although you can learn a lot by watching someone else do a job, you will never learn that job as well and as thoroughly as when you do it yourself.

Evaluating Your Work Experiences

You might find it helpful to reflect on your work experiences as you go through them. This process can help you figure out if the field you have chosen is right for you. Jot down whatever you can; below are some questions that can help.

1. What type of work is being done?

2. How is the work being done?

3. What sorts of things do you find fun? What do you find to be boring?

4. What kinds of suggestions do you have for a better workplace?

5. What additional training will you need to start up your own venture in this field?

Asking yourself these questions will help you think about and analyze the type of work you are doing. In addition, be careful not to neglect how you feel about the work you have been doing.

Internships

An internship can give you the opportunity to have a structured experience—combining both work experience and the development of new skills—in a field you are considering for your career. The work is often unpaid, although you can find positions with a stipend or an hourly rate of pay. The work may be part-time during an academic term or full-time when school is on break. Internships are invaluable for exploring career possibilities and gaining work skills valued in the marketplace.

Volunteering

Anyone can volunteer in practically any organization. While you don't get paid in a volunteer position, many people find it to be extremely rewarding work. Volunteering is a great way to help out an organization while learning about it and all the different levels of work that are involved.

One way to gain valuable experience in a field is "shadowing," or accompanying someone to his or her job to get a sense of the daily responsibilities.

Job Shadowing

Job shadowing occurs when you follow someone around at his or her job to see what that particular job is like. Job shadowing can be particularly beneficial when you think you have found something that is well-suited to your interests and capabilities, but you aren't quite sure if it's the right match for you. It often helps to see the day-to-day experiences of someone else to figure out if that field is the right one for you.

How do you find someone to job shadow? You may be lucky enough to have a friend or an acquaintance who can show you the ropes. Or, you might have to look a little harder. Talk to your guidance counselor about setting up a job shadowing experience, or do a little research of your own.

In addition to observing, be sure to ask as many questions as you can of the person you are with. You might want to find out how the person became interested in the work, how the field has evolved or changed, and what kind of training and experience are necessary. You also might want to consider what technical skills are necessary to perform the job well, and how they are used. In addition to technical skills, you should also notice how the person uses basic skills—such as writing, listening, and speaking—to be successful at the job. It also helps to take note of how the person you are shadowing uses people skills to work effectively with others in the workplace.

Also, pay close attention to whatever needs to be done as the person goes about his or her job. You can even offer to help; this will give you a more complete experience. You may also find it helpful to take good notes about the different components of the job, such as the work environment and the nature of interactions with others. Noting what you like about the job—and what you dislike—is also a good idea. And when your shadowing is done, don't forget to write a thank-you letter to the person you job shadowed. You may want to mention exactly what you found most helpful about the experience.

As you can see, there are many different ways you can learn about a variety of careers. Explore, learn, and have fun as you uncover what your interests are.

3

When the Timing Is Right

Timing is an important element when deciding to do most things, and when you are starting a company, timing is key. On the one hand, you have to figure out if it is the right time for you to get started on such a large project. You should make sure that you have ample experience and knowledge before you begin setting up your business.

Depending on your field, background, and resources, the right time for you may be when you are just out of college, or later on in life. Because you should know all that you can before you put all of your time and effort into launching a successful business venture, it is important not to rush your efforts. Additionally, the timing should be right for you in terms of finances and resources. Do you have the money and support you need to get your business off the ground? Most people find that starting a business costs much more money and involves many more resources than they originally thought.

Getting Started—A Big Leap

Let's say you have a great deal of experience, have done ample research, and have solid financial backing. However, are you emotionally ready to stand up to this challenge? It is not uncommon to realize mid-way through the start-up process that you aren't quite ready to make this kind of leap. You may decide to put off your decision or to progress more slowly than you had originally planned.

Perhaps you will decide to work full- or part-time in a corporation, using your spare time to work on your business until it gets off the ground. This may feel less stressful and overwhelming than dropping everything to start your own business. Or perhaps you will decide that because of the time and effort involved, you need to give up your job to focus on your business. Remember that everyone works at a different pace, and that different things work for different people.

Carla's Stationery Store

Carla was twenty-four when she decided to start her own stationery business.

"Ever since high school, I have dreamed about starting my own stationery venture," she says. "In college, I took business and economics courses to help me prepare for the financial aspects of running a business. And during the summers and on week-ends, I tried to do things that related to my interests. One year, I had a job working in a stationery store. And one summer, I did

Make sure that you have gained knowledge and experience before you begin setting up your business.

an internship at an interior design firm; another summer, I worked part-time in a small accounting firm. I chose all these positions so that when the time came, I would know exactly how to run my business."

When Carla turned twenty-two, she felt she was ready. She was able to save enough money from her part-time jobs to start her business, and she spent a long time doing research and talking to other entrepreneurs.

Unfortunately, the market wasn't right: unemployment was high, jobs were scarce, and she didn't think it was a good time to open her business.

"Times were tight for everyone," she says. *"I just didn't think it was worth the gamble to try something new when the economy wasn't right."* It was tough for Carla to put off her decision, but it turned out to be the right choice. *"I waited two years, just to be safe,"* says Carla. *"The economy was booming, people were spending more money, and it seemed like the right time to open my business. I did, and a couple of years later, it's doing great. And so am I!"*

In Carla's case, the timing was almost perfect to start her venture; she was financially ready, had plenty of experience, and had done a lot of research. But these factors aren't enough to ensure that the timing will be right. There are external factors that are important as well. When making any career decision, it is important to remember that your choices must fit into the realities of the working world. In other words, you should research whether there is consumer demand—meaning that people will want to use your services and have a need for what your business will provide.

Looking into Market Trends

You should also make sure that the labor market trends are in your favor. In other words, at certain times, depending on what economic conditions are like, some employment fields will enjoy more growth than others. As an example, in the 1990s, there was a technology boom during which computers and the Internet became extremely popular. This meant that there was a high demand for people with computer backgrounds and technical experience. Thus, this was a good time for people to start computer businesses and develop Web sites.

Geography Plays a Part, Too

Finally, you should make sure that the general economic conditions in the area where you are living are appropriate for what it is that you are trying to do. More specifically, Carla's stationery store might have a better chance in a city, rather than in a small farming town. Or, if the city has an abundance of stationery stores and the farming town has none, perhaps she would do better in the farming town. You should also make sure that

35

Books and periodicals can prove valuable to entrepreneurs researching a particular field.

there are people in your area who may be in the market for the services you are trying to provide. In other words, Carla's store might be great, but if no one is interested in or has a need for what she is trying to sell, then it is likely that her store will not do well.

You may be wondering how you can find out if the economic conditions are right for you. Do all the research you can. The following sources can be helpful to you:

1. **Career manuals.** Many manuals and books—which can be found in your local library or in a bookstore—will tell you about "projected outlooks" for certain fields. For example, you might find that in the computer field, the growth of business and the expected outlook for jobs has a "faster than average" growth of employment for at least the next three years. Or, you might find out that the jobs in a particular field are expected to diminish within the next five years. This type of information can help you plan what type of work will be in demand in the future.

2. **Specialized books.** Do further research by looking through books that are specific to your field and to your interests. These sources often comment on the outlook for particular fields, and what types of innovations and ideas are expected to crop up in the upcoming years, and so on. Many authors predict the things they feel might be "up and coming" in the next few

Entrepreneurs can take advantage of new occupational trends such as working at home, or telecommuting, when launching their businesses.

years. This type of information can help you think about the direction of your business.

3. **The Internet.** The Internet is a valuable source of information that contains the hottest and most current news available. Research the market conditions, economic conditions, and outlooks for certain careers in order to find out if this is a good time to begin a business, if you should wait, or if you should reconsider or adjust your plans.

4. **Newspapers and magazines.** Newspapers and magazines often run features on careers and the job market, and certain magazines publish features such as "The Top Ten Upcoming Careers." These types of publications are extremely worthy, especially since they are current. These sources will help you uncover market trends, hot careers, and which businesses are not doing so well.

A change in any of these factors has the potential to create new career opportunities or to lead to the elimination of jobs. It is up to you to gain a basic understanding of these trends so that you can adjust your career preparation and take advantage of emerging possibilities.

Occupational Trends

Occupational trends, which concern your role within a certain field, are another thing to keep in mind. As an example, if you are in the publishing industry, you can be a full-time or part-time employee of a publishing firm, or you can be a freelancer. Technological advances are also significant. One change due to the advent of high technology has been the increased number of people telecommuting (working from home). If telecommuting sounds interesting to you, you might consider setting up a business that enables you to work from home.

Timing Is Essential

Timing is extremely important when it comes to starting a new venture. It is important to note, however, that no matter how much research you do, or how stable the economy seems to be, things can change. You cannot be completely certain about some aspects of the market. However, by matching your strengths and interests with the needs of the field you are interested in, you will be able to fulfill your career goals while filling a niche in the labor market. You are making a big investment in preparing for your career, so make sure that your skills will be marketable in the future by keeping up with occupational and labor market trends.

4

Common Characteristics of Entrepreneurs

You may be wondering what types of skills or characteristics are necessary to be an entrepreneur. As you might imagine, people possess many different qualities that help them be successful entrepreneurs.

Important Skills to Have

Good Organizational and Time Management Skills

Being able to organize and manage your time well are invaluable skills in most types of work, but are perhaps even more useful to entrepreneurs. Because of the many things that are involved in starting a business, it is important to be organized and to budget your time appropriately. People who initially lack strong organizational skills, but who then try to improve their skills, often say that their lives are much easier afterwards.

Knowing How to Prioritize

Prioritizing means figuring out what is most important to do, and doing those tasks first. Many of us tend to first do the tasks that we enjoy or find easy. Knowing which tasks should come first—irrespective of how easy or fun they are—is an important quality to have. Putting off the tasks you don't want to do won't make them go away. It's often better to attack them first.

Knowing How to Set and Achieve Goals

Everyone works differently and has different styles and methods for achieving what he or she wants. But knowing how to set and achieve goals is an important quality for an entrepreneur. In terms of day-to-day functioning, it is helpful to have to-do lists that take into account your goals for the day—whether they are as simple as organizing your files or as complex as getting new clients.

It is also wise to set larger goals for yourself so that you have targets to work toward. When do you want to have something completed? Why is this goal important to you? What steps are you going to take to get yourself there? Keep in mind that nothing is set in stone; you can revise your goals, adjust your dates for doing them, or even prioritize them differently as you go on. No matter how often you change your plan, it is important that you have one in place and that you stick to it as best you can.

Good at Developing Solutions to Problems

While you may have a lot of support and help from family, friends, and contacts, it is important that you are able to come up with solutions on your own. You won't always have other people around, particularly when you have to make a fast decision. For example, let's say you have ordered some supplies for a client's project, but the supplies haven't come in yet. When you call the vendors, they tell you they are having shipping problems and your order will not be ready until next week. So what are you going to do? Being able to think of a variety of options on your own can make the difference between a successful result and losing a client over something that could have been prevented.

Ability to See the Big Picture

Because you will likely experience a few setbacks when you are starting your venture, it is important that you maintain the ability to see the big picture and to keep things in perspective. A mistake may seem huge at the time, but in the larger scheme of things, you may realize it's not such a big deal after all. Think of all the times you got upset about something and it turned out to not be as big of a deal as you had thought. Try to remember this when you are working and are starting something new.

Personal Characteristics

There are numerous personal characteristics that many entrepreneurs have in common. Some of these include:

1. **Enthusiasm and Energy.** Being enthusiastic and energetic are characteristics common to

Starting and running a business requires a great deal of organization and the ability to work on your own.

most entrepreneurs. Because of the effort, time, and hard work that goes into starting a new business, an enthusiastic demeanor and high energy level can help an entrepreneur get through the hard times and stay positive about the future.

2. **Ability to Deal with Stress Effectively.** Starting your own business often brings a great deal of stress. Because you are ultimately responsible for the fate of your business and how successful it is, it is important that you are able to deal well with the stress and complications that can exist. Successful entrepreneurs are able to handle stress well and do not tend to break down or give up when stress levels are high. In fact, many entrepreneurs even thrive in stressful situations.

3. **Ability to Ask for Help and Support.** When you are starting up your own business, why would this be important? Because no matter what the situation is or who is involved, we all need to be able to lean on others or ask for help from time to time. In a start-up, this is no different, and in fact it becomes more important. People who are not able to ask for help often burden themselves unnecessarily with tasks that they easily could have asked others to help out on.

4. **Ability to Work Well on Your Own.** Just as it is important to know when to be able to ask others for help, it is also important to be able

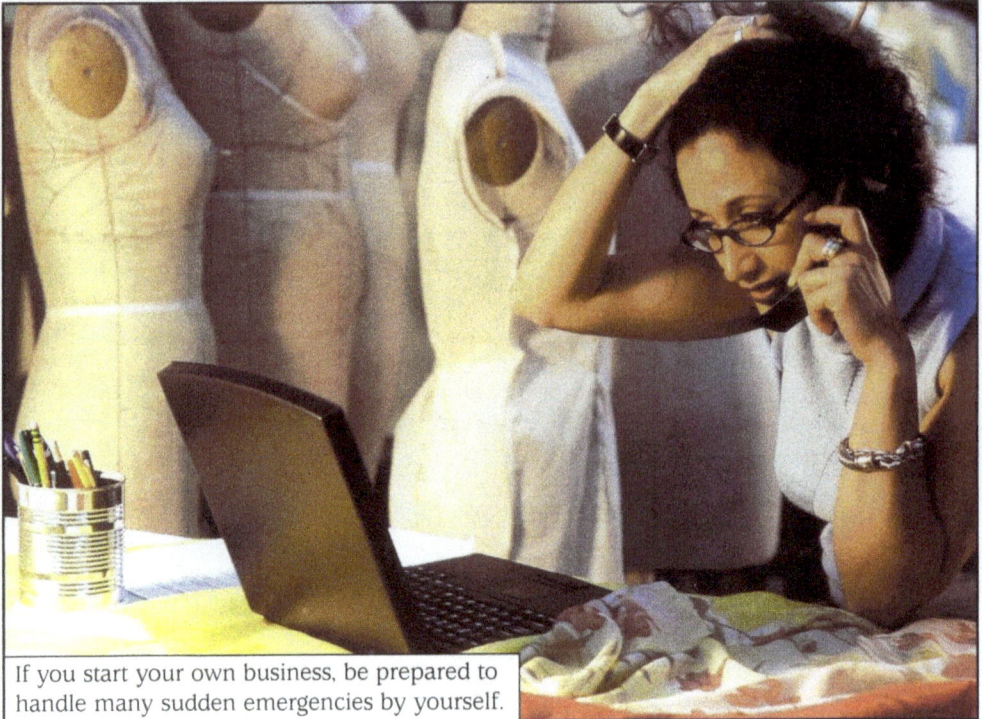

If you start your own business, be prepared to handle many sudden emergencies by yourself.

to work well alone, particularly when you are first starting your business. You should be prepared to spend many hours working on your business by yourself, especially in the initial stages. Thus, it is important to not only like working by yourself, but to do it well.

5. **Ability to Take Appropriate Risks.** Many entrepreneurs have become successful because they took an important risk, whether it was making a decision that was contrary to what everyone else said to do, or making a decision against logic or reason. You can be a successful entrepreneur by doing things by the book, but frequently success falls on those who take a few risks along the way.

Entrepreneurs also tend to possess a passion for the type of industry they are in. Unless you

46

are interested in most or all facets of a particular type of work, you may want to rethink starting a business within that field. Another attribute many successful entrepreneurs have is nonstop innovation and the ability to stay one step ahead of the competition. These skills will help your business stay fresh and will aid in keeping your customers interested.

5

The Importance of a Positive Attitude

Because there are so many different kinds of entrepreneurs, you may think that it would be impossible to think of some of the characteristics all of these people have in common, or to come up with a few different ways in which all entrepreneurs are alike. For example, how can you compare an individual who starts his own contracting business in Iowa with a person who designs clothing in New York? And how do you compare a nineteen-year-old entrepreneur developing computer software in his basement to a forty-five-year-old entrepreneur doing consulting work in many major cities? All of these details aside, the people who are drawn to being entrepreneurs tend to have at least one thing in common: optimism.

Optimism and the Entrepreneur

First of all, let's discuss optimism, or having a positive attitude. A person who is optimistic has the ability to be hopeful and positive. You may have heard the expression "Is the glass half empty or is it half full?" An optimistic person will see the glass as being half full—meaning that what is important is what we can see, and not what is missing.

How does optimism come into play when we think of the life of an entrepreneur? For one thing, optimistic entrepreneurs lay out clear goals for how they want their businesses to succeed. They tend to make realistic timetables and spend 50 percent or more of their time focused on achieving these goals.

Optimism Versus Pessimism

It is difficult to succeed while being a "pessimistic" entrepreneur. Pessimistic people are often focused on what can go wrong. While a little dose of realism is a useful thing, it is difficult to succeed when you are always expecting to fail.

Optimistic entrepreneurs have many things in common. For one thing, they tend to think of solutions. In other words, they focus on what they want to have happen as opposed to getting hung up on what is wrong. They remind themselves of the great possibilities that could occur, as opposed to worrying and second-guessing their choices. In short, optimistic entrepreneurs focus on how they want to grow their business and achieve their goals, not on how they might fail or what they will do when they fail.

Another thing to remember is that not only will an optimistic entrepreneur have an easier time getting a business off the ground, but his or her optimism will also affect the venture even after the

Entrepreneurs must have, or at least convey, optimism when running their businesses.

business is doing well. Consider the case of Manny, who was one of Ben's four employees.

Manny's Dilemma

"Ben had started up a gardening supply company, which was doing well and expanding at a rapid pace," says Manny. "He was used to putting long hours of work into the company, but when the company grew, he knew he would have to hire more people. That's when he brought me and three others on board."

"At first, it was a great experience," says Manny. He loved being a part of this successful young business and found the work challenging.

"But Ben was quite pessimistic, and his attitude affected the rest of us," he says. "As an example, one time we were experiencing delays in the orders for our shipments. They weren't huge delays, and it wasn't going to present too much of a problem, but Ben kept telling us what a disaster it was, and that he thought we would lose some of our customers over it. Of course, that never happened, but in the end, the damage was done. Ben had us so worried that we were going to lose customers, and that we were going to lose our jobs, that we knew we had to do something."

In the end, Manny and his coworkers sat Ben down for a little talk.

"After that, things improved," says Manny. "I don't think he completely stopped his negative thinking, but at least he didn't share it with us!"

Clear Vision

Optimistic entrepreneurs tend to have a very clear vision of what it is they want to achieve. Their goals are uncluttered with "what-ifs" and "buts," and instead of focusing on all the things that could go wrong, they work toward their vision with a positive outlook.

As we saw with Ben, one of the dangers of being a pessimistic entrepreneur is that your negative attitude can rub off on your employees and get in the way of their working toward their goals. As we have mentioned, being realistic is important, but successful entrepreneurs try to keep their realism balanced and positive. They set attainable goals and work toward them in the best way possible. Ben was able to start a successful business even though he tended to be pessimistic, but he might have had an easier time if he had thought more positively.

Being Responsible and Having Confidence

Another important attribute that optimistic entrepreneurs possess is that they tend to take full responsibility for all of their successes—and all of their failures. Whereas pessimists tend to blame other people when things go wrong, optimists accept that they may have made wrong choices and they move on from there. In the end, this is a

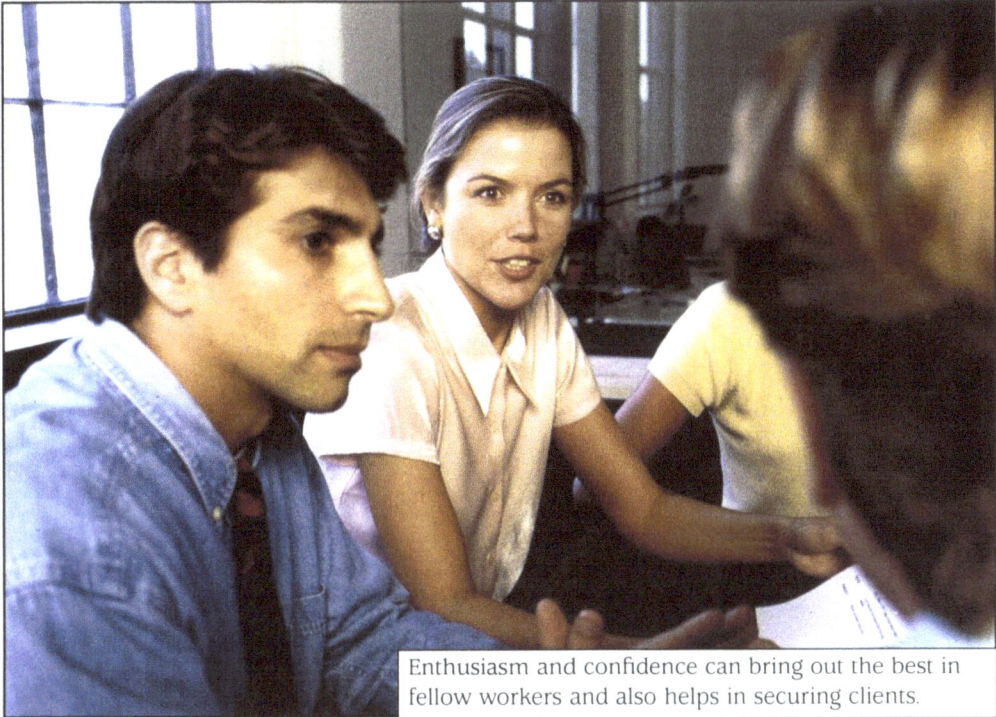
Enthusiasm and confidence can bring out the best in fellow workers and also helps in securing clients.

healthier way of operating, and since entre-preneurship usually involves both successes and mistakes, it is an incredibly important thing to keep in mind.

Finally, optimists tend to be more confident in what they do, and their confidence can rub off on those around them. A "can-do" attitude can inspire others to work harder and more effectively. Other people, such as potential customers, can recognize such a confident spirit and will probably be more willing to work with you if they can see that you have this attribute. Who wants to work with some-one who expects to fail? You guessed it: no one.

Keep Your Chin Up

The important thing to remember is to keep your chin up and to look at mishaps and setbacks as learning experiences. You will learn a seemingly infinite amount of information as you begin your new venture—try to absorb it all with excitement and energy. It won't always be smooth sailing, but running your own business will provide you with a multitude of lessons about work—and about life.

Glossary

business model Strategy and methodology for running a business.

business plan Specific outline detailing the intentions and goals of the business.

consumer demands Level of a particular need in the marketplace; e.g., the number of people who want a particular thing. If there is a high consumer demand for a product or service, then this means that many people want that product or service.

entrepreneur One who organizes, operates, and assumes the risk in a business venture in expectation of gaining a profit.

financial backing Amount of money that a person has for a particular venture. For example, if a person has strong financial backing to start his or her business, this means the person may have enough money to start the business and nurture it until it succeeds.

internship Job or program whereby a person, often a student, works for a relatively short period of time to get experience. Internships are often unpaid or offer a small stipend.

job shadowing Program where a person (the "job shadower") follows a working individual over a designated period of time (a few hours or a few days). This experience is intended to give the job shadower a firsthand look at what a particular job or field is like and what the day-to-day activities consist of.

mentoring Program whereby a subordinate learns from a wise and trusted teacher, counselor, or senior-level employee.

occupational trends Occupational trends are concerned with your role in a particular field. For example, if you are in the computer industry, there may be a large number of people who work in freelance positions within that field, or there may be a large number of people working for corporations.

optimism Disposition to expect the best possible outcome or to emphasize the most positive aspects of a situation.

volunteering To enter into a venture, often to provide service to a worthy cause or group, without being paid.

For More Information

In the United States

Distributive Education Clubs of America (DECA)
1908 Association Drive
Reston, VA 20191
(703) 860-5000
e-mail: decainc@aol.com
Web site: http://www.deca.org

Junior Achievement
One Education Way
Colorado Springs, CO 80906
(800) THE-NEW-JA
Web site: http://www.ja.org

National Foundation for Teaching Entrepreneurship
120 Wall Street, 29th Floor
New York, NY 10005
(800) 367-6383
e-mail: nfte@nfte.com
Web site: http://www.nfte.com

Students in Free Enterprise
1959 East Kerr Street
Springfield, MO 65803-4775
(417) 831-9505
Web site: http://www.sife.org

In Canada

Canada/British Columbia Business Service Centre
601 West Cordova Street
Vancouver, BC V6B 1G1
(800) 667-2272
(604) 775-5525
e-mail: askus@cbsc.ic.gc.ca
Web site: http://www.sb.gov.bc.ca

Women Business Owners of Canada
97 Spence Street
Winnepeg, MB R3C 1Y2
(888) 822-WBOC (9262)
Web site: http://www.wboc.ca

Young Entrepreneurs Association of British Columbia
3260 West 10th Avenue
Vancouver, BC V6K 2L2
(604) 730-7847
e-mail: info@yeabc.com
Web site: http://www.yeabc.com

Web Sites

digitalMASS at Boston.com
http://www.digitalmass.com

Entrepreneurs Information and Resources from
 About.com
http://entrepreneurs.miningco.com

Forum for Women Entrepreneurs
http://www.fwe.org

Teen Entrepreneur
http://www.teenentrepreneur.com

The Young Entrepreneurs Network
http://www.youngandsuccessful.com

Young Entrepreneurs' Organization
http://www.yeo.org

For Further Reading

Alaba, John O. *Starting Your Own Business and Making It a Success.* Chicago, IL: TFS Publishing, 1998.

Green, Meg. *The Young Zillionaire's Guide to Investments and Savings.* New York: The Rosen Publishing Group, Inc., 2000.

Kalahota, Ravi. *E-Business: Roadmap for Success.* New York: Addison-Wesley, 1999.

Kushell, Jennifer. *No Experience Necessary: The Young Entrepreneur's Guide to Starting a Business.* New York: Random House, 1997.

Maxye, Henry, and Henry Lou. *101 Tips for Running a Successful Home Business.* Los Angeles, CA: Lowell House, 2000.

Norman, Jan. *What No One Ever Tells You About Starting Your Own Business.* Chicago, IL: Upstart Publishing Co., 1999.

Pearce, James J. *Starting Your Own Business.* Woodinville, WA: Rhapsody Press, 1996.

Ridgway, Tom. *The Young Zillionaire's Guide to Buying Goods and Services.* New York: The Rosen Publishing Group, Inc., 2000.

Ross, Allison J. *Choosing a Career in Desktop Publishing*. New York: The Rosen Publishing Group, Inc., 2000.

Tiffany, Paul. *Business Plans for Dummies*. Forster City, CA: IDG Books Worldwide, 1998.

Turner, Patricia L. *How to Overcome the Fear of Starting Your Own Business*. Omaha, NE: Black Swan Press, 1991.

Tyson, Eric, and Jim Schell. *Small Business for Dummies*. Forster City, CA: IDG Books Worldwide, 1998.

Index

M

money/financial backing, 19, 21
    22, 31, 32, 34

N

networking, 23–25
new ideas, 10, 18, 37, 47
newspapers and magazines,
    16, 39

O

occupational trends, 39–40

P

part-time work, 23, 27, 32,
    34, 39
passion/desire, 10, 14, 46
people skills/interaction, 29, 30
pessimism, 49, 51–52
positive attitude/optimism, 45,
    48–53
prioritizing, 42

R

responsibility, taking, 52–53
risks, willingness to take, 46

S

skills,
    basic, 29
    developing, 26, 27
    organizational, 41
    technical, 29, 35
stress, dealing with, 45

T

technology boom, 10–12,
    35, 40
telecommuting/working from
    home, 40
time, managing your, 41, 49
training, 27, 29

V

volunteering, 23, 27

W

work experience, 10, 18, 23–26,
    27–30, 31, 32
    evaluating your, 26–27

About the Author

Lucy MacGregor is a freelance writer who has been published in various newspapers and journals, including *Le Monde, The Toronto Star,* and *The Montreal Gazette.* She lives in Manhattan with her new puppy.

Photo Credits

Cover photo © Frank Siteman/Index Stock; p. 2 © Michael A. Keller Studios Ltd/Pictor; p. 8 and 28 © Superstock; p. 11 © Ron Chapple/FPG International LLC; p. 15 © Randy Napier/Pictor; p. 16 © Stephanie Maze/Corbis; p.20 © Corbis; p. 25 © David Stover/Pictor; p. 33 © Telegraph Colour Library/FPG International LLC; p. 36 © Christoph Wilhelm/FPG International LLC; p. 38 © Steve Chenn/Corbis; p. 44 © Lisette LeBon/Superstock;p.46 © Barry Rosenthal/FPG International; p. 50 © Bob Krist /Corbis; p. 53 © Davis Stover/Pictor.

Design

Geri Giordano

Layout

Les Kanturek

www.ingramcontent.com/pod-product-compliance
Lightning Source LLC
Chambersburg PA
CBHW050910210326
41597CB00002B/79